I0605275

ESCARAMUZA

Constance Jaeggi

ESCARAMUZA

The Poetics of Home

GOST

USA

Angelina Sáenz

Moriré como una charra

En la tierra tenemos cosas materiales
pero cuando mueras
no puedes llevar nada contigo

Tú tienes que decidir que perdurará
¿Qué vas a pasarle a los tuyos?
¿A qué te aferrarás para siempre?

La cultura perdura
Escaramuza es cultura

Existe un dicho
Tú no naces charra,
pero te puedes convertir en una
y cuando dejes esta tierra
la dejarás como una charra

Mi abuelo fue sepultado como un charro
Voy a escribirlo en mi testamento
que a mí también me sepulten en mi traje de gala

Charrería es lo que me llevaré y lo que dejaré atrás

I will die as a charra

On earth we have material things
but you can't take any of that with you
when you die

You have to decide what is going to last
What will you pass on?
What will you hold onto forever?

Culture lasts
Escaramuza is culture

There is a saying
You are not born a charra
but you can be made into one
and when you leave this earth
you will leave as a charra

My grandfather was buried as a charro
I am going to write in my will
that I also need to be buried in my traje de gala

Charrería is what I will take with me
and what I will leave behind

Obstacle Queen

Give me all you've got
Nothing can stop me

My horse is sick
I'll borrow another one

I don't have a place to stay
I'll sleep in my car

I get stranded on the 15
with blown out tires
and my horses in the trailer
I will still find a way to make it to practice

I don't have a truck
I'll borrow it
from a perfect stranger
if I have to

I competed last year
without owning my own horse
I still don't own a horse!

Cancelling practice is never an option
I always figure it out

Reina de obstáculos

Dame todo lo que tienes
Nada puede detenerme

Mi caballo se enferma
Yo pido otro prestado

No tengo un lugar donde quedarme
Duermo en mi coche

Me quedé atorada en la 15
con los neumáticos reventados
y mis caballos en el remolque
Encontraré la manera de llegar
al entrenamiento

No tengo una camioneta
Pediré una prestada
a cualquier extraño
si tengo que hacerlo

Competí el año pasado
sin tener mi propio caballo
¡Aún no soy dueña de uno!

Cancelar nunca es una buena opción
Siempre me las arreglo

We talk with our eyes

My chestnut-coloured horse
gallops into the arena
I am side-saddle
my wide-brimmed embroidered sombrero
snug on my head

A high-neck green dress
balloons over my petticoat and pantaloons
I am ready

Our team of eight
performs a precise, synchronized routine
at full speed

Our horses turn inward from a wide circle
and charge into the centre
We closely pass each other
The slightest change in expression
communicates if anything is wrong
We cross in front of and behind each other
then erupt into partner turns

Thundering back to the perimetre

our choreography

flawless

Hablamos con nuestros ojos

Mi caballo color castaño
entra en la arena galopando
Yo monto al estilo amazona
mi sombrero bordado de ala ancha
ajustado a mi cabeza

Un vestido verde de cuello alto
se agranda sobre mis enaguas y bombachos
Estoy lista

Nuestro equipo de ocho
ejecuta una rutina precisa, sincronizada
a toda velocidad

Nuestros caballos giran hacia adentro desde
un amplio círculo y se lanzan hacia el centro
Nos pasamos estrechamente
El más mínimo cambio en nuestra expresión
comunica si algo está mal
Cruzamos delante y detrás la una de la otra
luego estallamos en vueltas en pareja

Irrumpiendo de nuevo hacia el perímetro

Nuestra coreografía

impecable

ire'ne lara silva

me llamo viento

nos anuncian *Valentina Covarrubias montada en Viento*
mi niña no se acobarda no saluda ni sonríe su rostro es orgulloso
y solemne sus hombros hacia atrás sus manos firmes en las
riendas sus ojos fijos en la gente reunida a nuestro alrededor
como diciendo mi nombre podrá ser Valentina pero debería
ser Valiente

su abuelo me talló de un viejo mesquite que imposible se extendía a través
de la propiedad de su rancho cantando todo el tiempo *caballo prieto*
azabache cómo olvidarte, te debo la vida carcajeándose
mientras cambiaba la letra sobre Pancho Villa y con sus propias
manos trabajaba la crin negra azabache de su caballo muerto
en la madera y la hacía mía

mi niña es muy joven decían para competir en un caballo de carne
y hueso aún faltan meses para su cumpleaños pero su corazón es el
de una guerrera ella trota y galopa para mí y hace que mi
nombre sea real ella sueña conmigo me ama cree en mí
cuando cabalgamos juntos ella es el viento yo soy el viento
somos el viento

—letra de la canción "Caballo Prieto Azabache" por José Albarrán Martínez

me llamo viento

they announce us *Valentina Covarrubias montada en Viento*
my girl does not cower does not wave or smile her face is
proud and solemn her shoulders are set back her hands steady on
the reins her eyes stare at the crowds gathered all around us as if to
say my name may be Valentina but it should be Valiente

her abuelo carved me from the old mesquite that stretched impossibly
across the land of his rancho singing all the while *caballo prieto*
azabache cómo olvidarte, te debo la vida laughing as he
changed the lyrics about Pancho Villa and with his own hands he
worked his dead horse's jet black mane into the wood and made it mine

my girl is too young they say to compete on a flesh and blood
horse her sixth birthday is still months away but her heart is a
warrior's heart she trots and gallops for me and makes my name a
true name she dreams of me loves me believes in me when we ride
together she is the wind i am the wind we are the wind

—song lyrics from "Caballo Prieto Azabache" by José Albarrán Martínez

no se olviden lo que quiere decir escaramuza

ellos ven elegancia ellos ven estilo dicen tradición dicen qué vestidos tan bonitos y Vogue dice
qué moda tan ornamentada debemos capturarla mostrársela al mundo es tan Mexicana y tan del
viejo Oeste tan vaquera   dios mío pero es que usan enaguas y bombachos dios mío
    y esas monturas laterales cómo es que permanecen sobre los caballos   y oh los
caballos son tan bellos sus crines fluyendo detrás de ellos   oh ya veo sus
caballos están bailando   es como natación sincronizada   oh es tan LINDO
                                        pero cuántos de ellos saben que
en inglés *escaramuza* es *combate*   que las mujeres montando a caballo levantando penachos
de polvo era una maniobra de guerra nacida de la estrategia y desesperación   ellos
necesitaban que las mujeres fueran feroces   que fueran rebeldes   que fueran bravas   que
fueran inteligentes   que montaran como demonios y distrajeran a los federales   hacerles creer
que había más soldados de los que había   para confundirlos para implicarlos   mientras
sostenían sus armas en sus brazos y acechaban a la muerte en sus ojos

no se olviden de lo que quiere decir escaramuza

they see elegance they see style they say tradition they say que vestidos tan bonitos and Vogue
says what ornate fashion we must capture it show it to the world it is so Mexico and so Old West
so Cowboy   omg are they wearing petticoats and bloomers omg   and those sidesaddles
how do they stay on the horses   and oh the horses are so beautiful their manes streaming
behind them   oh I see   their horses are dancing   it's like synchronized
swimming oh it's so PRETTY
                                        but how many of them know that in
English *escaramuza* is *skirmish*   that women riding on horses sending up plumes of dust
was a battle manuever born of strategy and desperation   they needed the women to be fierce
to be defiant   to be brave   to be clever   to ride like devils and divert the federales to
make them think there were more soldados than there were   to confound them to engage
them   while cradling their weapons in their arms and holding death in their eyes

no era lo más cruel que había dicho

pero fue suficiente para robar todo el aliento de mis pulmones
cualquier muchacha no defendida por su madre
cualquier mujer no protegida por su padre hermano o esposo
esa muchacha esa mujer
era carne de cualquiera

nocarnenovíctimanocarnenovíctimanocarnenovíctima
me defiendo me protejo este mundo me aceptará como soy
o reharé el mundo ser mujer no me despoja de poder
no tengo miedo no viviré con temor no me acobardaré no vacilaré mi corazón es un machete
si quiero montar a horcajadas si quiero competir si quiero usar mi fuerza si quiero vivir sin jamás
bajar la mirada entonces lo haré

it wasn't the cruelest thing he ever said

but it was enough to steal all the breath from my lungs
any girl not defended by her mother
any woman not protected by a father brother or husband
that girl that woman
was anyone's meat

notmeatnotvictimnotmeatnotvictim
i defend myself i protect myself this world will take me as i
am or i will remake the world being a woman doesn't render me powerless
i am not afraid i will not live in fear i will not cower i will not flinch my heart is a machete
if i want to ride astride if i want to compete if i want to use my strength if i want to live without
ever lowering my eyes then i will

born a woman and died a man

Malaquías Amelia de Jesús
Robles Ávila was born in 1889
Colonel Amelio Robles died in
1984 at age 24 he changed his
name in the mouths of men at
gunpoint then fought with Zapata
through 70 battles commanding
thousands of soldiers

Robles was not the only one to
name himself not the only one to
put on men's clothing and say
mine not the only one then or
now or even longer ago what is it
to cling so anxiously to what is a
man and what is a woman and
what is a man's life and what is a
woman's life

we all of us seres humanos are
called to our lives to the truths of
our beings Robles found himself
on the battlefield and even after
the revolution kept finding
himself on battlefields of
prejudice and violence and
erasure but he never surrendered
and that is the lesson he never
surrendered and died victorious

nació mujer y murió como hombre

Malaquías Amelia de Jesús
Robles Ávila nació en 1889
Coronel Amelio Robles murió en
1984 a los 24 cambió su nombre
en las bocas de los hombres a
punta de pistola luego luchó con
Zapata a lo largo de 70 batallas
comandando a miles de soldados

Robles no fue el único que se
nombró a sí mismo ni el único
que se puso ropa de hombre y
dijo *mío* ni el único entonces o
ahora o hace mucho tiempo que
cesó de aferrarse con tanta
ansiedad a lo que es ser hombre y
lo que es ser mujer y qué es la
vida de un hombre y qué es la
vida de una mujer

todos nosotros seres humanos
somos llamados a nuestras vidas
a las verdades de nuestros seres
Robles se encontró a sí mismo en
el campo de batalla y aún
después de la revolución siguió
encontrándose a sí mismo en las
batallas del perjuicio la violencia
y cancelación pero nunca se
rindió y esa es la lección que
nunca se rindió y murió
victorioso

ire'ne lara silva

what the ghosts of las adelitas say in the afterlife part 1

we didn't have time for ribbons or petticoats or
high necked dresses no time for sidesaddles or
single spurs no one else to saddle or feed or care
for our horses we practiced when we could and
paid the price of not learning with falling with
bruises with broken bones with our lives with
the lives of our loved ones
we taught each
other when we did not know what we could eat
beyond frijoles and nopales portulaca and the
seeds of the mesquite we taught each other what
was medicine what roots what leaves what seeds
what poultices what prayers in whatever
languages we knew we trusted our children to
each other knowing we might not return
men
rewrite history with impunity they will remake
repaint reshape us say they loved us and fought
for us they will lighten our skin and change our
features highlighting hips and nipples and red
red lips or they will make us all into virgin
madonnas protecting mexicanidad
but our red
red blood spilt on the ground does not know how
to be silent we did what we had to do to
survive then and later in this life in the afterlife
or the life before the stories are not dead stories
never die we will speak our piece the living can
be silenced the dead cannot

lo que dicen los fantasmas de las adelitas en el más allá parte 1

no tuvimos tiempo para listones o enaguas o
vestidos de cuello alto ni tiempo para monturas
o espuelas individuales nadie más para ensillar
o alimentar o cuidar a nuestros caballos nosotras
entrenábamos cuando podíamos y pagábamos el
precio de no aprender con caídas y moretones
con huesos rotos con nuestras vidas con las
vidas de nuestros seres queridos
nos enseñábamos
las unas a las otras cuando no sabíamos qué
podíamos comer más allá de frijoles y nopales
portulaca y las semillas del mesquite nos
enseñábamos lo que era medicina qué raíces qué
hojas qué semillas qué emplastos qué oraciones
en cualquier lenguaje sabíamos que nos
confiábamos a nuestros hijos sabiendo que
quizás no regresáramos
los hombres
reescriben la historia con impunidad ellos nos
reharán nos repintarán nos remoldearán dirán
que nos amaban y que luchaban por nosotras
nos blanquearán la piel y cambiarán nuestras
facciones acentuando caderas y pezones y labios
rojos rojos o nos convertirán a todas en vírgenes
madonas protegiendo la mexicanidad
pero nuestra sangre
roja derramada en el suelo no sabe cómo
callarse hicimos lo que teníamos que hacer para
sobrevivir entonces y después en esta vida en la
otra vida o en la vida anterior las historias no
han muerto las historias nunca mueren nosotras
diremos nuestra parte a los vivos pueden
silenciarlos a los muertos no

lo que dicen los fantasmas de las adelitas en el más allá parte 2

pero cómo pudimos dejar nuestros hogares
preguntaron cómo pudimos empuñar las armas
preguntaron cómo pudimos dejarlo todo
preguntaron por qué necesitan preguntar
nuestros padres nuestros hermanos nuestros
esposos nuestros hijos fueron asesinados
nuestras madres hermanas hijas fueron violadas
qué otra cosa había por hacer mas que aprender
a apretar el gatillo aprender a usar un cuchillo
aprender a recibir cada día sabiendo que podría
ser el último ver nuestras manos cubiertas de
sangre y nunca rendirse no había tiempo para
mentiras no había forma de negar lo fino del
muro entre vivir y morir dejamos nuestros
hogares para hacer lo que pudiéramos dejamos
nuestras vidas para luchar por lo que amábamos
una mujer que se convierte en un arma jamás
olvida lo que es

what the ghosts of las adelitas say in the afterlife part 2

but how could we leave our homes they asked
how could we take up arms they asked how
could we leave everything behind they asked
why do they need to ask our fathers our brothers
our husbands our sons were killed our sisters
our mothers our daughters were raped what else
was there to do but to learn to pull the trigger to
learn to use a knife to learn to greet each day
knowing it might be the last to see our hands
covered in blood and never give up there was no
space for lies no way to deny the thinness of the
wall between living and dying we left our
homes to do what we could we left our lives to
fight for what we loved a woman who becomes
a weapon never forgets what she is

lo que dicen los fantasmas de las adelitas en el más allá parte 3

los amamos los cuidamos mientras dormían
adoramos la subida y la caída de sus pechos nos
inclinamos cerca para inhalar el aire que
exhalaban mientras dormían apartamos el
cabello de sus frentes
veneramos la
tibieza de sus labios el peso de sus cuerpos sus
manos callosas tiernas y urgentes en turnos
vivimos eones de éxtasis manteniéndolos cerca
olvidando sangre y batalla y temor
entonces y después nos llamaron
rameras y perdidas por tener amantes por falta
de anillos y ceremonias en pequeñas iglesias las
mujeres decentes no vivían como nosotras
decían
pero qué es decencia y qué es respeto y a
quién le importa lo que digan cuando la muerte
nos puede llevar en cualquier momento cuando
la muerte podía y así lo hizo
nosotras luchamos por la
libertad luchamos por tierra luchamos por la
vida nosotras luchamos y amamos luchamos
porque no había otra manera no luchar era morir

what the ghosts of las adelitas say in the afterlife part 3

we loved them we watched over them while
they slept adored the rise and fall of their chests
leaned in close to breathe the air they exhaled
brushed the hair from their brows
worshipped the
warmth of their lips the weight of their bodies
their calloused hands tender and urgent in turns
lived eons of ecstasy held close forgot blood and
battle and fear
then and later they called us
whores and perdidas for taking lovers for the
lack of rings and ceremonies in little churches
mujeres decentes did not live as we lived they
said
but what is decency and what is respect
and what does it matter what they say when
death could take us at any moment when death
could and did take us
we fought for freedom we
fought for land we fought for life we fought we
loved we fought because there was no other way
to not fight was to die

Angelina Sáenz

La Hebilla

No me importa el dinero del premio;
Yo sólo quiero la hebilla

The Buckle

I don't care about the prize money;
I just want the buckle

Puedes darnos las gracias después

Hermano charro
¿Te das cuenta
de que es gracias a la escaramuza
que tienes un público?

Nuestras presentaciones
son la parte más anticipada del espectáculo
Si sólo fueran los hombres
tendrías tan solo tres personas en las gradas

Es verdad, nos dan 8 minutos
y a ustedes 8 horas
pero créeme
los niños, padres, hermanos, y hermanas
en las gradas
vienen especialmente por esos 8 minutos

¿Dónde más podrías ver deportividad tan elegante?

You can thank us later

Brother charro
do you realize
that it is because of escaramuza
that you have an audience?

Our performances
are the most anticipated part of the show
If it was just the men
you'd have three people in the stands

It is true, we get 8 minutes
and you get 8 hours
but trust me
the kids, parents, brothers
and sisters in the stands
come especially for those 8 minutes

Where else can you see
such elegant sportsmanship?

You are prettier when you are quiet

I am a feminist who loves my sport
and the machismo in charreria often gets to me

To be clear
I am not talking about my father, brothers
husband or trainer
who respect, encourage and support me

I am talking about the men
who want me
to keep my mouth shut

I am supposed to sit pretty
and accept
that I don't have a voice

I tell myself to get used to it
like white noise in the background

and then something reminds me again
of how women
are second-class citizens in this sport
and I want to fight back

My dad tells me not to say anything
He does not want to give anyone
the opportunity to disrespect me

The escaramuzas need to come together
If we combine the strength
and unity of our teams
we will get the vote

I hope and pray
that one day
we will get past this
and we will have a voice

Calladita te ves más bonita

Soy una feminista que ama su deporte
y el machismo en la charrería a veces me harta

Para ser más clara
no estoy hablando de mi padre o mis hermanos
esposo o entrenador
quienes me respetan, motivan, y apoyan

Hablo de los hombres
que quieren callarme

Debo sentarme y verme bonita
y aceptar que no tengo una voz

Me digo a mí misma
que debo acostumbrarme
a ser callada como una sombra

Pero entonces, algo me vuelve a recordar
que las mujeres son ciudadanas de segunda clase
en este deporte
y yo quiero luchar contra esto

Mi padre me aconseja que no diga nada
Él no quiere darle a nadie
la oportunidad de faltarme al respeto

Las escaramuzas necesitan unirse
Si todas combinamos nuestra fuerza
y la unidad en nuestros equipos
nos ganaremos el voto

Espero y rezo
para que un día
dejemos esto atrás
y todas tengamos voz

Cómo hablarle al liderazgo machista

1. Piensa antes de decir algo
2. No digas absolutamente nada
3. No te pongas a la defensiva o seas argumentativa
4. Ignóralos cuando te digan que estás a la defensiva o argumentativa
5. Simplifícalo, dibújalo si tienes que hacerlo
6. Halágalos o hazles creer que es su idea
7. Toma nota cuando dejen de escuchar
8. Anótalo todo y léelo directamente del papel
9. Dilo y ya
10. Acepta cuando nada cambie

How to talk to the machista leadership

1. Think before you say anything
2. Don't say anything at all
3. Don't be defensive or argumentative
4. Ignore when they say you are defensive and argumentative
5. Dumb it down, draw pictures if you have to
6. Compliment them or make them think it's their idea
7. Notice when they stop listening
8. Write it all down and read it off of a paper
9. Just get it over with
10. Accept when nothing changes

There is no difference between us

You were born in México
I was born in the United States
There is no difference between us

You speak Spanish
I speak English
and always need a translator
There is no difference between us

My mom is white
Your mom is Mexican
There is no difference between us

You just show up to practice
and then go home
I have to do everything myself
before, during and after practice
There is no difference between us

You own many horses
I don't own a horse
There is no difference between us

You compete with the horse
that you trained with all year
I am on a horse
that I met three days ago
There is no difference between us

When we are fixing to do a beautiful show
Sitting on our horses in our beautiful dresses
Adrenaline shooting through our body
and the love for our sport in our hearts
There is no difference between us

No existe ninguna diferencia entre nosotras

Tú naciste en México
Yo nací en los Estados Unidos
No existe ninguna diferencia entre nosotras

Tú hablas español
Yo hablo inglés
y siempre requiero de un traductor
No existe ninguna diferencia entre nosotras

Mi madre es blanca
Tu madre es mexicana
No existe ninguna diferencia entre nosotras

Tú te presentas a los entrenamientos
y después te vas a casa
Yo me presento a los entrenamientos
y hago todo sola antes, durante, y después
No existe ninguna diferencia entre nosotras

Tú tienes muchos caballos
Yo no tengo ni un solo caballo
No existe ninguna diferencia entre nosotras

Tú compites con el caballo
con el que entrenaste todo el año
Yo estoy sobre un caballo que apenas conocí hace tres días
No existe ninguna diferencia entre nosotras

Cuando nos preparamos para brindar una bella presentación
Montadas en nuestros caballos y nuestros bellos vestidos
La adrenalina disparándose a través de nuestros cuerpos
Y el amor por nuestro deporte en nuestros corazones
No existe ninguna diferencia entre nosotras

Angelina Sáenz

Look at our boots and spurs!

No
I don't dance horses
I am not a mariachi
I am not a baile folklorico dancer
I am not the half-time show
or the intermission
I am not just a pretty woman
sitting on a horse
that is standing still

I am a charra
with extraordinary riding skills
I am sitting side-saddle
drenched in my own sweat
buried in a heavy, layered dress
while I control
1,000 pounds of muscle beneath me

I am enacting a dangerous
mathematically precise routine
at full velocity

I have fallen off of my horse
suffered concussions
broken bones, been dragged
and trampled on

So, the next time you see a woman
dressed like me

Look for the boots and spurs
and then you will know

who I am

¡Mira nuestras botas y espuelas!

No
Yo no hago bailar a caballos
Yo no soy un mariachi
No soy una bailarina de ballet folclórico
No soy el espectáculo de medio tiempo
o el intermedio
No soy tan solo una mujer bonita
montada en su caballo
que está quieto

Soy una charra
con extraordinarias destrezas de equitación
Voy montada al estilo amazona
empapada en mi propio sudor
enterrada bajo un vestido pesado y en capas
mientras controlo
1,000 libras de músculo debajo de mí

Estoy ejecutando una rutina peligrosa
y matemáticamente precisa
a máxima velocidad

Me he caído de caballos
arrastrada y pisoteada
He sufrido de contusiones cerebrales
y roto huesos

Así que la próxima vez que veas a una mujer
vestida como yo

Busca las botas y espuelas
y vas a saber

quién soy

Hay que respetar el atuendo

Si vas a usar este vestido
tienes que observar las reglas

Sí, son conservativos y estrictos
pero esta es nuestra historia y herencia

Por ejemplo
siempre debes llevar enaguas
El cuello del vestido debe ser alto
Nada que muestre tus hombros
Tu cabello no puede ir suelto
Debe ser recogido en la nuca
sujetado por un listón
y atado al estilo mariposa

Me siento ofendida
cuando tú no observas estos requisitos
Este atuendo tiene una larga tradición
Estamos representando nuestra cultura

Dress pet peeves

If you are going to wear this dress
you have to respect the rules

Yes, they are conservative and strict
but this is our history and heritage

For example
You should always wear a petticoat
Your dress should be high-neck
Nothing off the shoulders
Your hair cannot be down
It should be gathered at the neck
held by a ribbon
tied in a perfect butterfly bow

I am offended
when you don't observe the requirements
This attire has a long tradition
We are representing our culture

Padre

Gracias
por comprarme el vaporizador
para mi vestido
que tú siempre me acusas
de no planchar

Gracias
por recoger el vestido
que dejé en el garaje
y colgarlo
en el guardarropa impermeable

Gracias
por entrenar a los caballos
y por asistir a todos los ensayos
y competencias

Cuando miro
tu cara sonriente en las gradas
me motiva

Quiero que te sientas orgulloso de mí

Dad

Thank you
for buying me a steamer
for the dress
that you always accuse me
of not ironing

Thank you
for picking up the dress
that I left in the garage
and hanging it up
in the waterproof garment bag

Thank you
for training the horses
and for being at the practices
and competitions

When I see
your smiling face in the stands
it motivates me

I want to make you proud

ire'ne lara silva

lo nuestro

lo cierto es   una hermandad
nacida de luchar y soñar y entrenar

lo cierto es   este devenir
un cuerpo un corazón una mente un espíritu
corriendo y girando y rodando

lo cierto es   fue un regalo
de la tierra   un regalo que vivió en más de
una tierra   un regalo que cruzó y volvió a cruzar
descruzar y deshacer fronteras

lo cierto es   que nos habíamos hecho
hermanas de cabalgar que estábamos creciendo
juntas como una familia que se extendía y seguía
extendiéndose que nuestros hijos estaban creciendo
juntos criados por tías y caballos

lo cierto es   que hay cosas
en la vida que no pueden renunciarse
porque renunciarlas sería entregar quienes somos
y rendirse jamás ha sido una opción
esta es la vida esta es la vida
esta es nuestra más verdadera vida

lo nuestro

it was the truest thing to say   a sisterhood
born of struggling and dreaming and training

it was the truest thing to say   this becoming
one body one heart one mind one spirit
running and whirling and wheeling about

it was the truest thing to say   that it was a gift
from the earth a gift that lived on more
than one land a gift that crossed and recrossed
and uncrossed and unmade borders

it was the truest thing to say   that we had
been made riding sisters that we were growing
up together like a family that kept branching
and branching that our children were being
raised together mothered by aunts and horses

it was the truest thing to say   that there
are things in life that can't be renounced
because renouncing them is to surrender
who we are and surrendering has never
been an option this is life this is life
this is our truest life

machetona

me llamaron por querer ponerme un traje de charro por querer montar a horcajadas por no desear límites *lesbiana* lo escupieron no sólo los hombres pero también las mujeres pero qué importa a quien yo desee a quien yo ame tradición dicen tradición significa que una mujer debe llevar puesto un vestido una mujer debe ser una dama una muchacha debe montar al estilo amazona porque un caballo no debería quitarle su virginidad una mujer no debe mostrar que es fuerte o capaz o valiente dicen pero y si un hombre quisiera ponerse un vestido esperando que yo retroceda horrorizada pero digo que el mundo no se acabaría si un hombre se pone un vestido el mundo no se acabaría si amo a quien yo ame el mundo no se acabaría si digo que este lugar también a mí me pertenece el mundo no se acabaría si vivo como digo que debo vivir

machetona

they called me for wanting to wear the traje de charro for wanting to ride astride for wanting no limits *lesbian* they spat out not just the men but also the women but what does it matter who i desire who i love tradition they say tradition means a woman must wear a dress a woman must be a lady a girl must ride sidesaddle because a horse should not take her virginity a woman must not show she is strong or able or clever or brave they say but what if a man wanted to wear a dress expecting me to shrink back in horror but i say the world will not end if a man wears a dress the world will not end if i love who i love the world will not end if say this place belongs to me too the world will not end if i live as i say i must live

escaramuza india

Sangre del indio que calla
Que llora, que ama
Que sabe sufrir
—José Arturo Rodríguez González

como los americanos
decimos que los indígenas están muertos
son sólo historias sólo ancestros
no viviendo no prosperando no creando respirando existiendo
aunque hay pirámides
y estatuas de Cuauhtémoc y retratos de Benito Juárez
para decirnos quiénes somos
rostros morenos con el nopal en la frente
como los americanos
reclamaremos lo europeo
a costa de lo indígena
La Federación Mexicana de Charrería
sólo reconoce
escaramuza charra
quiero ver a las mujeres montadas a pelo
y cantándole a sus caballos

escaramuza india

Sangre del indio que calla
Que llora, que ama
Que sabe sufrir
—Jose Arturo Rodriguez Gonzalez

like the americanos
we say the indigenous are dead
are only stories only ancestors
not living not thriving not creating breathing being
even though there are pirámides
and statues of Cuahtémoc and portraits of Benito Juárez
to tell us who we are
brown faces con el nopal en la frente
like the americanos
we will claim the european
at the price of the indigenous
La Federación Mexicana de Charrería
only recognizes
escaramuza charra
i want to see the women riding bareback
and singing to their horses

lo de ser mexicana y americana

no somos partes
no donde nacimos
no lo que otros piensen
somos nuestra sangre
somos nuestra historia
somos lo que amamos

inmigrantes de primera generación
segunda tercera cuarta quinta sexta
generación no importa
sólo nuestros corazones importan
sólo nuestro orgullo
y nuestro anhelo importan

lo de ser mexicana y americana

we are not parts
not where we were born
not what others think
we are our blood
we are our history
we are what we love

immigrant first generation
second third fourth fifth sixth
generation does not matter
only our hearts matter
only our pride
and our yearning matters

what the lienzo prays every time the sun rises

they name me arena
but i am a canvas
and each movement
made by a charro
an escaramuza
a horse a bull
any beast
is a
stroke of paint

may the horses
run as if winged
may the bulls
be fierce as thunder
may the charros
be as ardent as the sun
may the escaramuzas
reveal their indomitable hearts

when this day is done
may everything
that happened here
linger
in memory
sport become art
both
eternal
and
ephemeral

lo que el lienzo reza cada vez que sale el sol

me nombraron arena
pero soy un lienzo
y cada movimiento
ejecutado por un charro
una escaramuza
un caballo un toro
cualquier bestia
es un
trazo de pintura

que los caballos
corran como si tuvieran alas
que los toros
sean tan feroces como el trueno
que los charros
sean tan ardientes como el sol
que las escaramuzas
revelen sus corazones indomables

cuando este día se acabe
que todo
lo que aquí sucedió
persista
en la memoria
que el deporte se convierta en arte
ambos
eternos
y
efímeros

ire'ne lara silva

cruce y remolino

después de todo que no es esto la vida cruce cruce remolino remolino
no mueras no lastimes a nadie en esto yo veo a las adelitas levantando polvo
burlando ejércitos en esto yo veo mi vida cuasi accidentes
y el placer de acelerar del peligro de la vida acentuada
todo depende del control de qué tan cerca estamos a la destrucción
al caos esto es
vida y belleza dragados desde el borde difuminado entre victoria y dolor
gruñidos severos y el golpeteo de sus rítmicos cascos

cruce y remolino

after all isnt' this what life is cross cross whirl whirl don't die don't
hurt anyone in this i see las adelitas raising dust fooling armies in this
i see my life near misses and the pleasure of speed of danger
of life made sweet everything depends on control everything depends
on how close we are to destruction to chaos this is
life and beauty dredged from the blurring edge between victory and pain
harsh grunts and the drumming of rhythmic hooves

el abanico

nos enseñan la belleza de la rosa
la serenidad de lo suave y lo quieto
la austeridad de estrellas plateadas en un cielo invernal
el ascenso de voces hacia alturas intocables
las imágenes y las esculturas
que no podemos imaginarnos han sido hechas por manos humanas

raras veces nos enseñan la belleza
del cuchillo giratorio captando la luz
del día que nunca repetirá
el asombro de sus corazones resonantes
caballo y jovencita caballo y mujer
disfrazando una fuerza tremenda

aquí crearemos la belleza
de lo crudo de lo vivo de las bestias
diremos que hemos visto vestidos elaborados
y espuelas plateadas individuales
caballos con capas brillantes
caballos con crines relumbrantes

quizás nunca hablemos de la belleza
que vimos ese día todos esos días
los caballos galopeaban a
sólo pulgadas
el uno del otro y las faldas
volaban en el viento y los rostros
de las mujeres sus rostros indomables

el abanico

we are taught the beauty of the rose
the serenity of the soft and the still
the austerity of silver stars in a winter sky
the soaring of voices to untouchable heights
the images and the sculptures
we can't imagine human hands making

we are rarely taught the beauty
of the spinning knife catching the light
of the day that will never repeat
the awe of their thundering hearts
horse and girl horse and woman
disguising tremendous strength

here we will create the beauty
of the raw of the alive of the beasts
we will say we saw elaborate dresses
and single silver spurs
horses with shining coats
horses with luxurious manes

we may never speak the beauty
we saw that day all of those days
the horses galloping only inches
away from each other and skirts
flying in the wind and the faces
of the women their indomitable faces

las historias de los caballos

qué dicen los caballos de los lienzos qué historias se cuentan uno al otro dónde nacieron lo que les contaron que serían sus destinos y si esas historias resultaron ser o no ser ciertas qué dicen los caballos de quienes los han amado qué entrenadores qué jinetes qué espectadores con qué premios secretos los alimentaron quién los estrechó muy cerca cuántas lágrimas brindaron refugio qué historias de las multitudes y el griterío y los aplausos qué historias de la música qué historias de quienes vivieron y murieron y quién fue vendido y quién fue regalado qué historias contaron de la vida después del lienzo o acaso ellos como nosotros no piensan sobre el futuro sólo piensan en el presente sobre la tarea el reto frente a ellos lo que les han enseñado y en lo que derramarán sus corazones mientras el día es tibio y el sol brilla y el lienzo está llamando

the stories of horses

what do the horses of the lienzos say what stories do they tell each other where they were born what they were told their destinies would be and whether or not those stories turned out to be true or not what do the horses say of who loved them what trainers what riders what owners what spectators what secret treats they were fed who held them close how many tears did they give refuge to what stories of the crowds and the shouting and the cheering what stories of the music what stories of who lived and died and who was sold and who was gifted what stories do they tell of life after the lienzo do they like us not think of the future only think of the now of the task the challenge before them what they have been taught and what they will pour their hearts into while the day is warm and the sun is shining and the lienzo is calling

Angelina Sáenz

Al caballo que lo logró en sólo tres días

Tres días antes de la competencia
Limpy se lastimó
y no podía competir conmigo

Me ofrecieron otro caballo

Este caballo
nunca había tenido una jinete montada al estilo amazona
Nunca había participado en una rutina

No se llevaba bien con los otros caballos
y no le interesaban los ejercicios de repetición
A veces simplemente rehusaba moverse

Trabajar con él era un riesgo
No todos los caballos son caballos escaramuza
pero hablé con él
Le di las gracias por trabajar conmigo
Le hice muchos elogios y le entregué mi confianza

Ese año yo gané
con ese caballo al azar
que tuve que entrenar en tres días

To the horse who pulled it off in three days

Three days before competition
Limpy got hurt
and could not perform with me

I was offered a new horse

This horse
never had a side-saddle rider
He had never been in a routine

He did not get along with the other horses
and did not appreciate the repeat drills
Sometimes, he simply wouldn't move

Working with him was a gamble
Not all horses are escaramuza horses
but I talked with him
I thanked him for working with me
I gave him lots of praise and assurance

I won that year
on that random horse
that I had to train
in three days

I am always apologising

to everyone
because I am always at practice
and never around

People send me invitations
even though they know
I won't attend

Sometimes, I feel so guilty
that I drive to Idaho at dawn
to attend a family event
and then drive back to Oregon
in the afternoon
to be at practice in the evening

I'm so tired when I'm driving
and I question my sacrifice

Yesterday, my prima pulled me aside
I've missed so many of her gatherings
I thought she was going to scold me
but she told me how proud she is of me
She admitted
she doesn't understand what I do
but is inspired
by my dedication and discipline

Moments like this
keep me going

Siempre estoy disculpándome

con todos
porque siempre estoy entrenando
y nunca estoy disponible

La gente me envía invitaciones
aun sabiendo
que no asistiré

A veces me siento tan culpable
que manejo hacia Idaho en la madrugada
para asistir a un evento familiar
y luego me regreso a Oregón
por la tarde
para estar en los entrenamientos por la noche
Me siento muy cansada mientras manejo
y cuestiono mi sacrificio

Ayer, mi prima me habló a solas
Me he perdido muchas de sus reuniones
Pensé que me iba a regañar
pero me dijo lo orgullosa que estaba de mí
Me confesó
que no entiende lo que hago
pero se inspira
en mi dedicación y disciplina
Momentos como este me animan a continuar

Esto es un estilo de vida, no un pasatiempo

Nosotras somos universitarias
recién casadas
tenemos hijos
tenemos recién nacidos
somos propietarias de viviendas
y dueñas de negocios

Nosotras pagamos por todo
de nuestros propios bolsillos
viviendo de cheque en cheque

Nos prestamos dinero
Nos ayudamos con gasolina
Compartimos nuestros caballos
Nos compramos sombreros
Reemplazamos nuestros aretes

Entregamos todo lo que tenemos a escaramuza

Esto no es algo que hacemos por placer
Esta es nuestra vida

This is a lifestyle, not a hobby

We
are college students
are newly married
have children
have newborns
are homeowners
and business owners

We pay for everything
out of our own pocket
Many of us live paycheck to paycheck

We lend each other money
We put gas in each other's car
We share horses
We buy each other's sombreros
We replace each other's earrings

We give everything we have to escaramuza

This is not what we do for leisure
This is our life

Four Generations

There is a framed photograph of my grandmother
She is a young woman, sitting on a horse, vestida de china
I have another photo of my grandfather
at five years old, dressed as a charro

My Mexican father did not introduce me to this sport
My white mother did
He was a horse jockey
She was an escaramuza
Horses have always been in our family

Today, my husband and I
both perform in charrerías

We are teaching our son and daughter
Our son has started to compete
My daughter is still too young
Charrería is our gift to them

I love when I see grandpa dressed up as a charro
and then I see my parents dressed up and riding
and you see the grandkids participating
and I ask myself

Is there another sport
where four generations
ride together?

Cuatro generaciones

Hay una fotografía enmarcada de mi abuela
Mujer joven montada sobre un caballo, vestida de china
Tengo otra foto de mi abuelo
a los cinco años, vestido de charro

Mi padre mexicano no me introdujo a este deporte
Mi madre blanca lo hizo
Él era un jockey
Ella era una escaramuza
Los caballos siempre han sido parte de mi familia

Hoy, mi esposo y yo
nos presentamos en charrerías

Estamos enseñando a nuestro hijo e hija
Nuestro hijo ya ha comenzado a competir
Mi hija aún es demasiado pequeña
Charrería es nuestro obsequio para ellos

Me encanta cuando veo a mi abuelo vestido de charro
y luego veo a mis padres vestidos y cabalgando
y ves a los nietos participando y me pregunto

¿Existe otro deporte
donde cuatro generaciones
cabalgan juntas?

20 21
EMUSA

Escaramuza, the Poetics of Home

Escaramuza. The word means 'skirmish' in English, and it is both a competitive equestrian team sport in the rodeo tradition of *charrería* (the sport and art of being a charro), and the name given to the women who compete. Each team consists of eight escaramuzas executing precisely choreographed routines on horseback, riding sidesaddle and all while dressed in stunningly ornate Victorian-era formalwear. Each team is a bevy of horsewomen in bright, high-necked gowns stitched with lace and ribbons, frothy petticoats and pantaloons, boots and sombreros. These are fierce women armoured in beauty.

Escaramuza is a unique sport, part ballet and part cavalry maneuvers and something all its own: a dazzling display of skilled horsewomanship, art and power. Their competitions are easily the most captivating of a charreada. Eight minutes of spectacle, a feminist fairytale, a curious juxtaposition of aggressively genteel feminine visuals and the escaramuzas' grit and skill as equestrian competitors.

Escaramuza flourishes in Mexico and has grown exponentially in the United States. Young Latinas all over the nation are investing themselves in a sport that champions heritage and tradition and allows them to be daring, bold and fearless.

Yet, what we see in the arena is not nearly the whole story. To talk about escaramuza is to talk about the origins of lore, identity and a long history of women heroically striving for their place as competitors in their own right, within charrería.

Charrería is a rodeo sport intrinsically tied to Mexican cultural identity, or *lo Mexicano*. The sport arose from the hacienda system, or cattle ranching culture, of colonial Mexico. A *charreada* is an event featuring riding and roping competitions based on branding events, roundups, bronc busting and other ranching culture activities. Prior to the Mexican Revolution, these events were informal contests between neighbouring haciendas. In the post-revolution era, the end of the hacienda system coalesced in a desire to i) preserve charrería traditions and ii) create a kind of nationalistic narrative around the charro, the idealised Mexican man—*un doble caballero*—both a gentleman and a skilled horseman. Established as the official national sport of Mexico in the 1920s, charrería fosters patriotism, the patriarchal family system and a romanticised view of Mexican identity.

Escaramuza marks the greatest progress women have made in this male-dominated sport. Prior to 1953, only men competed. Some historians say the charro Luis Ortega created the escaramuza tradition in 1950, after observing a team of cowboys and cowgirls perform at a rodeo in Houston, Texas. Ortega later established his own precision riding team of children—both boys and girls. Other sources indicate escaramuza began at Rancho del Charro in Mexico City, in 1952. What is certain is that the first escaramuza teams were actually coed. However, boys were soon banned from escaramuza, as the performances were considered *demasiado femenino*, or 'too feminine.'

Escaramuzas were first allowed to perform—though not compete—in charreadas in 1953, the year Mexico granted women the right to vote. By 1958, escaramuza was an all-female exhibition. This first wave of escaramuzas performed at the discretion of the individual chapters of the charro associations, as ornamentation or extra entertainment, not on par with the charro events.

As a newly-created addition to the sport, escaramuza needed a matching narrative to complement the iconic charro mythos within the nationalistic framework of charrería. Escaramuza borrowed heavily from the history of *soldaderas*, women who accompanied, cared for and even fought alongside the men of the Mexican Revolution.

Within the charrería, and in greater Mexican culture, the more sanitised elements of soldaderas were emphasised and idealised. Fanciful tales surround these figures: women warriors, skilled horsewomen, who would act as decoys on the battlefield, female revolutionaries, who were lovely and brave, but also chaste and genteel. They were called *adelitas*, named for Adelita, Pancho Villa's legendary soldier-sweetheart, who fought alongside him. In the cultural imagination, soldaderas were akin to 20th century Valkyries, or modern day *amazonas*, but within a strictly coded femininity and proper moral conduct.

In reality, soldaderas were often poor women of both rural and urban backgrounds. Many of them were *mestizas* (those of mixed racial and cultural heritage), but a large percentage were indigenous. Soldaderas were camp followers, often working as foragers, cooks, nurses and yes, at times, impressive fighters, but also lovers and even whores. Some women were even leaders of army units. Since revolutionary armies did not have formal ranks, women officers were called *generala* or *coronela*, giving rise to the popular corrido 'Coronelas' a favorite choice for escaramuza choreography. A number of soldaderas took on masculine identities, dressing as men and adopting male names. In other words, the soldaderas contained, as do women today, a kaleidoscope of experiences, diverse lives and backgrounds.

Though escaramuza adopts the more wholesome, romanticised aspects of the soldaderas, their true history is a legacy for the women who compete in the sport, in both Mexico and the US. This complex history lies beneath the rich pageantry of the escaramuza image, as does the will to participate fully within charrería, as competitors. These women are riders and horsewomen, not ornaments.

Through the decades, through the development of teams across Mexico and the US, and its rising popularity, a second wave of escaramuza emerged. Women continued the tradition, organising and petitioning, actively pursuing the validity of their art and passion. Escaramuza became a recognised competitive event in 1992.

This third wave of escaramuza, a sport with judges and regulations on par with charro events, has gained traction in the US. There are teams in Texas and California, but also Iowa, Minnesota, Wisconsin and many others. Each year, more than 100 teams compete in the US, vying for the chance to compete at the national escaramuza competition in Mexico.

Like charros, escaramuzas work year-round to perfect their skills, learn the choreography routines, execute each formation and work together as a team. They display as much tenacity as their male counterparts, caring for and feeding their horses, training with them, driving long hours to competitions, hauling trailers and of course, figuring out how to pay for their gear and tack, as well as the incredible escaramuza outfits. The surge of popularity for US escaramuza teams has not translated to sponsorships, as it has in Mexico.

The US teams hold bake sales, car washes, sell hot plates of food, hold raffles. They face the unique challenges of crossing borders without their horses and having the additional challenge of competing on rented or borrowed horses who do not know the routines and are unfamiliar with their riders. Through it all, these women are devoted to their sport and to experiencing this unique part of their heritage. It is a bond of sisterhood that lasts a lifetime.

03 *Paola, Sandra, Stephanie, Stefanie, Caren, Yasmeen and Emma*
Escaramuza Erandi
Buckley, Washington, 2023

05 *Harina*
Escaramuza Tierra Azteca
Midlothian, Texas, 2023

09 *Mariana*
Escaramuza Villa De Guadelupe
Brownsville, Texas, 2023

11 *Cynthia*
Escaramuza Charras de Agua Santa
Del Valle, Texas, 2023

12 *Anita*
Escaramuza La Victoria
Joshua, Texas, 2023

15 *Laura, Alexis, Valeria, Mariana and Priscilla*
Escaramuza Charra Villa de Guadelupe
Brownsville, Texas, 2023

17 *Darline*
Escaramuza Flor de Aguileña
Lakewood, Colorado, 2023

19 *Nataly, Jennifer, Guadalupe, Yoana, Cynthia and Citlallie*
Escaramuza Zacatecanas
Des Moines, Iowa, 2024

21 *Emma, Stephanie and Lizeth*
Selección de Oregon
Mulino, Oregon, 2024

23 *Valentina*
Selección IME
Riverside, California, 2023

24 Escaramuza Erandi
Buckley, Washington, 2023

33 *Emily, Maria Jose and Kimberly*
Escaramuza Charras de Agua Santa
Del Valle, Texas, 2023

35 *Candy and Alexia*
Coronelas de Illinois
Lockport, Illinois, 2023

37 *Fabiola*
Esacramuza Sueño Dorado
Nampa, Idaho, 2024

39 *Jazmin*
Escaramuza Tierra Azteca
Midlothian, Texas, 2023

40 *Paola*
Escaramuza Erandi
Buckley, Washington, 2023
41 *Jennifer*
Escaramuza La Victoria
Joshua, Texas, 2023

43 *Patricia and Jasmin*
Escaramuza Dinastia Campiraña
Henderson, Colorado, 2023

45 *Valentina, Samantha and Katie*
Escaramuza Reinas Del Valle
Nampa, Idaho, 2024

47 *Paloma, Fabiola, Natalie, Emma and Estefania*
Escaramuza Sueño Dorado
Nampa, Idaho, 2024

48 *Alexia*
Escaramuza Dinastia Campiraña
Henderson, Colorado, 2023

57 *Gabriela*
Escaramuza Rayenari
Scottsdale, Arizona, 2024

59 *Analuisa and Jessica*
Escaramuza Las Norteñas
Canutillo, Texas, 2024

61 Escaramuza Tierra Azteca
Katy, Texas, 2023

63 *Paola*
Escaramuza Erandi
Buckley, Washington, 2023

65 *Yamilex, Naomy and Katie*
Escaramuza Reinas Del Valle
Nampa, Idaho, 2024

67 *Xiomy, Camila, Sarah and Emily*
Escaramuza Lirios de Tennessee
Kingston, Georgia, 2024

68 *Patricia*
Dinastia Campiraña
Bennett, Colorado, 2023

71 *Jasmin*
Dinastia Campiraña
Bennett, Colorado, 2023

72 *Perla*
Dinastia Campiraña
Bennett, Colorado, 2023

81 *Verónica*
Escaramuza Las Norteñas
Canutillo, Texas, 2024

83 *Alejandra*
Escaramuza Esquetzalli
Des Moines, Iowa, 2023

85 *Brenda, Naiomy and Carolina*
Escaramuza Flor de Aguileña
Lakewood, Colorado, 2023

86 *Miranda*
Escaramuza La Victoria
Joshua, Texas, 2023

87 *Laura*
Escaramuza Charras Villa de Guadelupe
Brownsville, Texas, 2023

89 *Gisele, Paloma and Eileen*
Escaramuza Nueva Illusion
Bennett, Colorado, 2023

91 *Marisol, Melanie, Nathaly and Stacy*
Escaramuza Charra Azteca
Manor, Texas, 2023

93 *Yadira and Lizette*
Escaramuza Quetzalli
Katy, Texas, 2023

95 *Estefania*
Escaramuza Sueño Dorado
Nampa, Idaho, 2024

96 *Patricia and Perla*
Escaramuza Dinastia Campiraña
Henderson, Colorado, 2023

105 *Michele*
Escaramuza Lucero Lindo
Katy, Texas, 2023

107 *Yadira*
Escaramuza Quetzalli
Katy, Texas, 2023

109 *Isabella, Alexia, Claudette and Anali*
Selección IME
Riverside, California, 2023

111 *Casandra, Jacqueline and Cheyenne*
Escaramuza Sagrado Corazón de Jesus
Brighton, Colorado, 2023

112 *Cassandra, Cythia and Anira*
Escaramuza Charras Villa de Guadelupe
Brownsville, Texas, 2023

115 *Jesenia, Amelia, Samantha and Areatana*
Escaramuza Reinas Del Valle
Nampa, Idaho, 2024

116–117 *Emily*
Escaramuza Charras de Agua Santa
Del Valle, Texas, 2023

119 *Itzel*
Escaramuza Coronelas de Illinois
Manhattan, Illinois, 2023

121 *Ana, Analuisia and Jessica*
Escaramuza Las Norteñas
Canutillo, Texas, 2024

Escaramuza
First published in 2025
by GOST Books, London

info@gostbooks.com
gostbooks.com

Edited and designed by GOST:
Rossella Castello, Katie Clifford, Gemma Gerhard, Justine Hucker,
Allon Kaye, Eleanor Macnair, Claudia Paladini, Ana Rocha

Printed in Italy by EBS

British Library cataloguing-in-publication data. A catalogue record of this book is available from the British Library.

ISBN 978-1-915423-96-2